TANWA

The story of a five-year-old living with sickle cell!

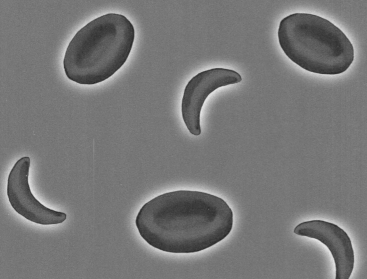

Written by Dr. Raolee
Illustrated by Aranahaj Iqba

love Dr. Raolee

Dedication

This book is dedicated to my two beautiful angels – Tara and Mimi.

I thank God every day for giving me the gift of motherhood.

You both give me a reason to be a sickle cell gladiator.

I love you.

Special thanks

A special thanks to all my friends and family that contributed to the process of completing this amazing book. It was not an easy task writing about the pain of sickle cell, but I know it is something that I need to do to contribute to our community to help give support and hope.

Tanwa is a five-year-old girl, and an only daughter.

She has two older brothers and two younger brothers.

Tanwa was born with a medical condition known as Sickle Cell Disease.

Occasionally, Tanwa becomes sick and feels a lot of pain in her body.

Whenever this happens, her doctors say she is having a crisis.

Let's meet Tanwa so she can tell us how sickle cell affects her.

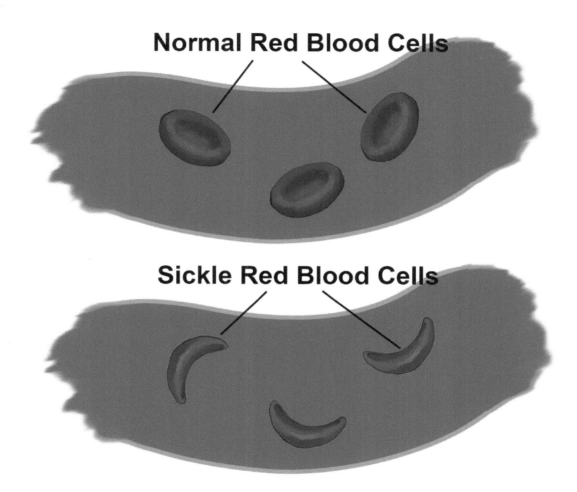

Hi there! My name is Tanwa, and I am a terrific five-year-old.

I have a mistake in my blood which makes me sick.

But, the good thing is that when I am sick, I don't pass it to others.

My sickness is not contagious like a cold, a cough, the flu, or COVID.

However, it is very painful whenever I have a crisis

I was born in Nigeria, West Africa.

I live in a bungalow with my happy family.

A bungalow is the same as a one-story house.

Our house has lots of unique, bright, and beautiful flowers.

We also have a giant, wooden swing outside.

My family is very large; my cousins, aunties, uncles, and friends always come over to visit.

My big brother, Yoola, likes books and is always reading.

Sometimes he reads to me, and that makes me happy.

I am learning to read, and I can now say all my alphabet.

I can even blend the sounds.

My big brother, Yemi, loves to play soccer with my little brother Yinka.

I like playing with them too because it's a lot of fun!

Most times I can't join the fun for long because I may get tired.

Then the pain could start, which might lead to another crisis, and that's no fun!

I like to play with my baby brother, Yusuf, and make him laugh.

When I tickle Yusuf or make a silly face, he laughs and laughs.

That makes me laugh too.

My mummy always says laughter is the best medicine.

But she still wants me to take all my medicine!

My baby brother, Yusuf, cries all the time.

The only time he is quiet is when he is asleep or when he is eating.

When I cry, it is because I am having a crisis.

The pain does not let me eat or sleep.

Only the pain medicine my mummy gives me puts me to sleep.

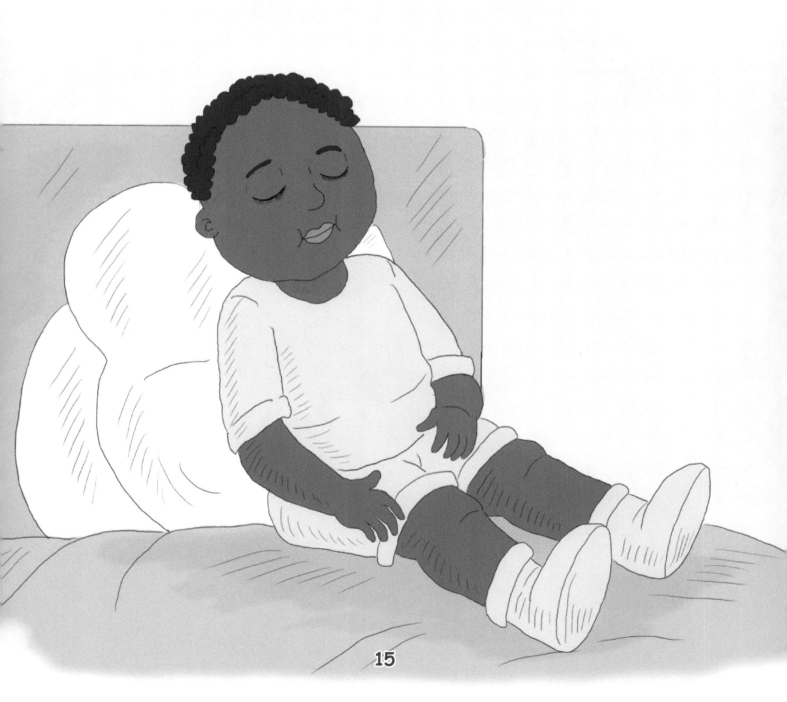

I love all my brothers because they make me feel special, especially when I am sick with sickle cell crisis.

When I have a crisis, I may have pain in my hands, legs, back or chest.

My brothers sit by my bedside to cheer me up!

But they are not allowed to be too loud because noise makes my pain hurt more.

My mummy said the noise has a vibration and it makes my pain hurt more.

So, when I am sick, I like to listen to soft music, and I pray and ask God to make me better.

My mummy always prays, and she tells my brothers to also pray for me.

I know God loves me because He always answers our prayers and makes my pain go away.

My mummy likes to pray, and she teaches us all to pray.

She tells us we are special and that she loves each of us.

She also likes to sing, and she tells us to count our blessings.

Mummy reminds my brothers to always be gentle with me.

"Why?" my brothers ask.

"Is it because she is a girl?"

"No," my mummy replies.

"It is because she has sickle cell."

23

"What is sickle cell?", I asked my mummy one day after a crisis.

"And why am I the only one who has it?"

My mummy explained to me that sickle cell is an inherited disease caused by gene mutation.

My mum has a trait of the gene, and so does my dad.

I got one trait from mum, and one from dad, and two traits causes sickle cell.

When the sickle-shape red blood cells get blocked in the veins, it causes pain in my body.

Sometimes I get so tired and cold. My mummy said the sickle red blood cells are high and my round red blood cells are low and this makes me - 'ANNAMIK'!

When the body does not have enough round red blood cells, then the oxygen level is low and this reduces the amount of energy and heat throughout the body, making the person anemic and tired. But when the sickle-shaped red blood cell gets clogged, that causes pain.

Sometimes I become very thirsty. My mummy says I am DEEHIDATED! So, I must drink a lot of water.

My doctor tells me that people with sickle cell are advised to stay well hydrated by drinking lots of water. If they do not, then the red blood cells become sickle, sluggish and can easily stick together and get clogged. That might trigger a crisis.

When I have a crisis, I get pains in one part of my body that may gradually flow to other parts. I may have pain in my hands, legs, back or chest.

The worst is when the pain comes to my chest and radiates everywhere – at the same time.

When I am in crisis, I burst into tears and scream in agony, "Mummy!!"

I try my very best to ignore the ache in my back. But the pain gets worse and worse and the throbbing in my back feels like I am being pounded by a hammer.

Boom! Boom!! Boom!!!

"Arrgggkkkkkk" I fall to the floor, curling into the fetal position. My cries of agony stop everyone in their tracks. My mummy rushes over to me and wraps her arms around me. Whimpering painfully, I cling to her as she picks me up and takes me into the bedroom to see what she can do to stop my pain.

I cry and cry and cry because of the pain. This makes my mummy worried and sad. She starts to pray, then gives me pain medication. Then she rubs a gooey white stuff on me, this keeps me warm and helps to soothe the pain. This stuff smells like menthol, and it tickles my nose. Finally, she gives me a hot water bottle to place where there is pain, and all this helps with the pain.

But sometimes the pain refuses to stop, so she takes me to hospital where the doctors and nurses can take care of me.

When I am sick, I sometimes play games on my mummy's phone, or I watch cartoons on the television. This makes me laugh and laugh.

When I laugh, I feel better than when I cry.

My mummy always says laughter is the best medicine.

People with sickle cell disease are not always sick. They can live normal productive lives. Most of the time, you cannot even tell that they have this condition except in some extreme cases.

As I said earlier, when I am fine, I like to play soccer with my brothers, or read a book to my baby brother, Yusuf. Sometimes my cousins visit, and we all have fun playing jump rope or hide-and-go-seek.

I also enjoy playing with dolls with my cousin. We braid our dolls' long hair.

My favorite food is rice and fried plantains . . . we call them doh doh.

My favorite things help me not feel so sad when I am not well.

I fall sick more than my brothers or my cousins, especially if I am cold, tired, or dehydrated.

I take different medication every day to help me. I do not like taking medicines, but I know I must because they help me. The only one I like is Folic Acid.

I don't know if you also sometimes get sick like me.

If you do, it is important to listen to your parents, take all your medicines even the yucky ones.

Drink plenty of water, eat healthy and go to bed early so you give your body time to heal

Then you will be fine and ready to play.

Next time I will tell you much more about myself and sickle cell genes.

Remember to laugh and be happy because laughter is the best medicine.

About the Author

Dr. Raolee is a 54-year-old sickle cell warrior, but she likes to refer to herself as a sickle cell gladiator because sees herself as more than a conqueror. Dr. Raolee is an educator, and she teaches robotics and engineering. She has successfully developed Robotics and Steam programs in various schools in America and the Middle East. Dr. Raolee has a doctorate degree in educational leadership and management.

Her parents discovered she had sickle cell when she was two years old and they were told she will not live to be 10 years old but she has defied all odds.

Dr. Raolee is passionate about helping others with sickle cell and she takes part in several sickle cell advocacy programs. Her series on Tanwa is inspired by her journey with sickle cell.

Dr. Raolee's wish is to share love, joy, and hope with people affected by sickle cell. One of her favorite quotes is – laughter is the best medicine. Everyday, she asks herself – have you laughed today? If the answer is no, then she will find something to make her laugh.

Dr. Raolee has two beautiful daughters ages 26 and 22.

Glossary

ANNAMIK - The way Tanwa pronounces anemia

Anemia – Deficiency of red blood cell

Anemic – Symptoms seen when a person has low red blood cells

Dehydrated – Deficiency of water in the body

Folic Acid – One of the medicines used for sickle cell management

Gene mutation – A change in a gene formation that may cause a disease/disorder.

Gooey white stuff – Products made with menthol to help relieve pain

Hot Water Bottle – A soft rubber container to keep hot water safe, but used to help reduce pain

Inherited disease – A disease that occurs in a person due to the genes they acquired from each parent.

Normal Red Blood Cell – Round shaped blood cells that carry oxygen around the body

Sickle-shaped Red Blood Cells – Crescent shaped blood cells that is deficient in oxygen, moves sluggishly and gets clogged in the blood vessels.

Sickle Cell Disease – Inherited blood disorder that affects every aspect of a person's life.

References

Mayo Clinic – www.mayoclinic.org

CPSIA information can be obtained
at www.ICGtesting.com
Printed in the USA
LVHW070800210522
719388LV00017B/71